A Kalmus Classic

L.
MILDE

FIFTY CONCERT STUDIES

Opus 26

FOR BASSOON

K 02132

50 CONCERT STUDIES
for bassoon
BOOK I

№ 1.

L. Milde, Op. 26.

3

№ 2.

Tempo I.

№ 3.

Adagio.

8

№ 4.

Allegretto.

9

№ 5.

№ 6.

Allegretto.

14

№ 7.

16

№ 8.

Allegretto.

№ 9.

№ 10.

Presto.

Fine.

p D.C. al Fine.

№ 11.

№ 12.

24

№ 13.

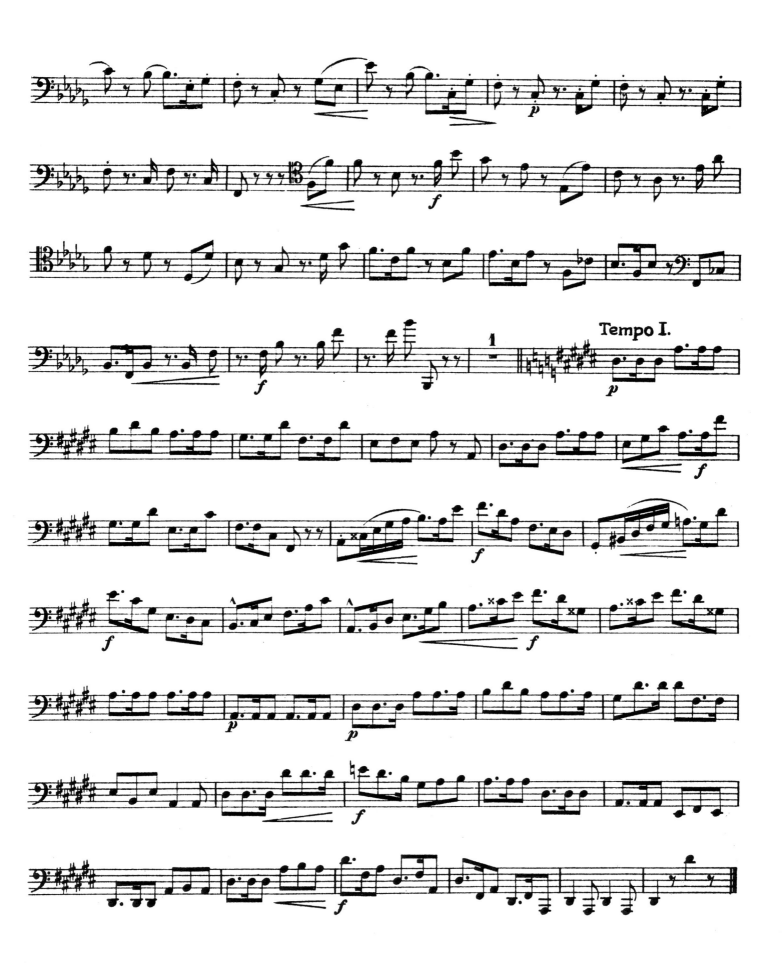

Tempo I.

№ 14.

27

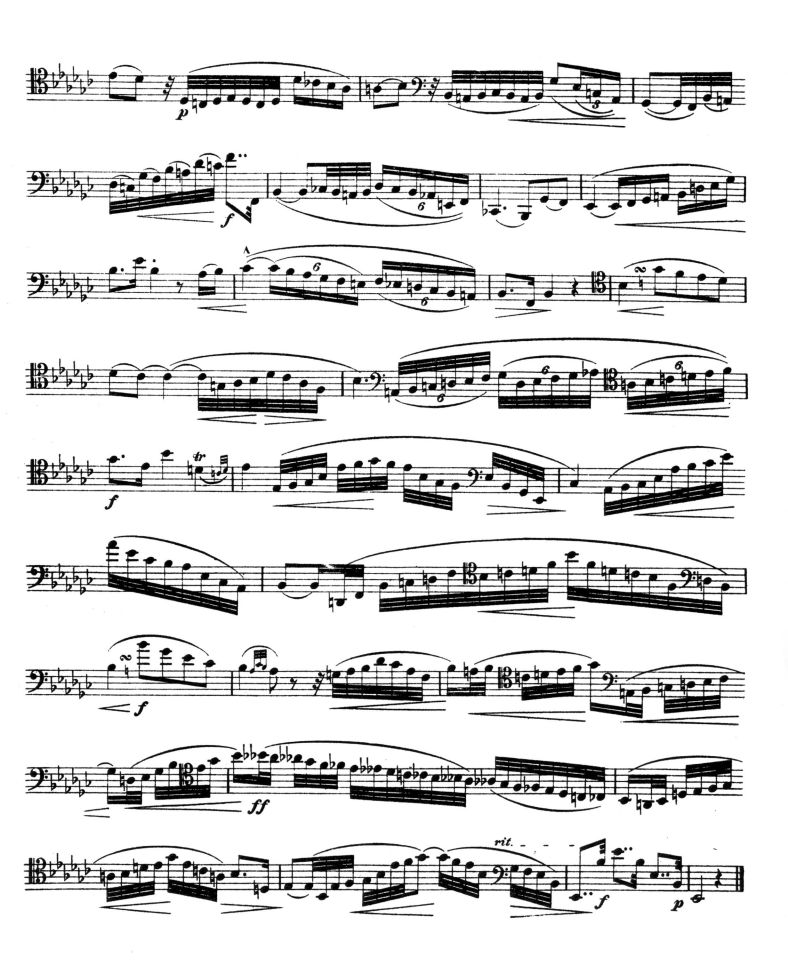

28

№ 15.

№ 16.

Allegretto.

Meno.

Tempo I.

№ 17.

34

№ 18.

35

№ 19.

Allegretto.

Tempo I.

38

№ 20.

Adagio cantabile.

39

№ 21.

№ 22.

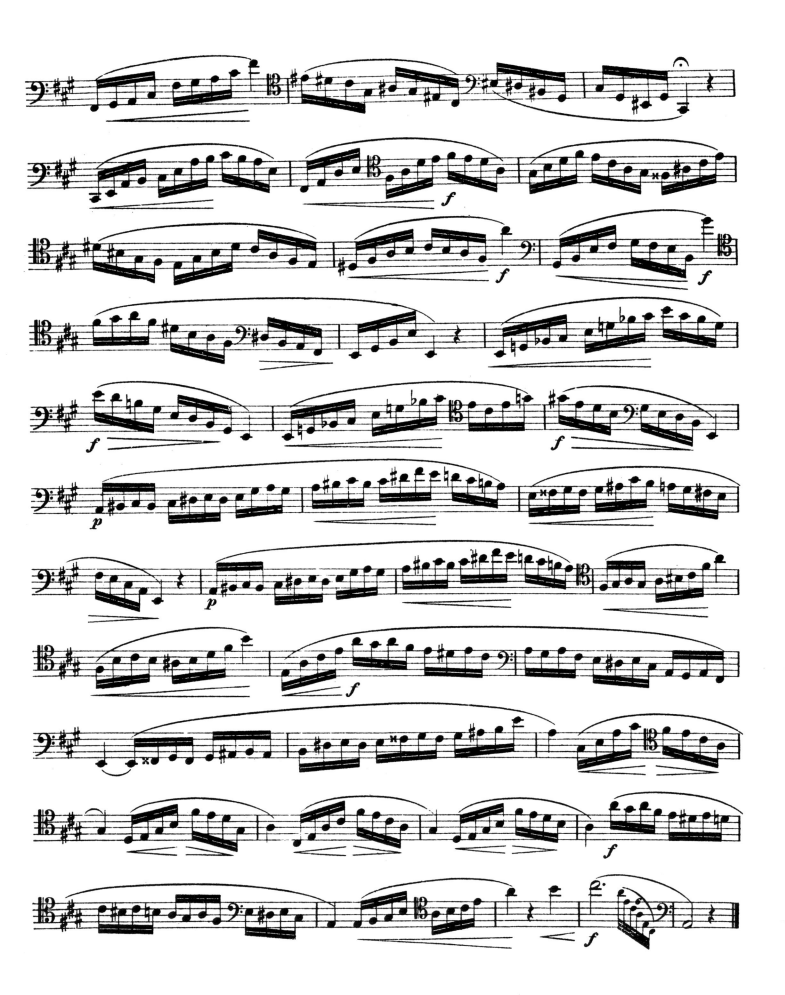

44

№ 23.

№ 24.

48

№ 25.

Tempo I.

50

Allegretto.

26.

28.

Allegretto.

54

Allegretto.

29.

57

58

Scherzo.

31.

59

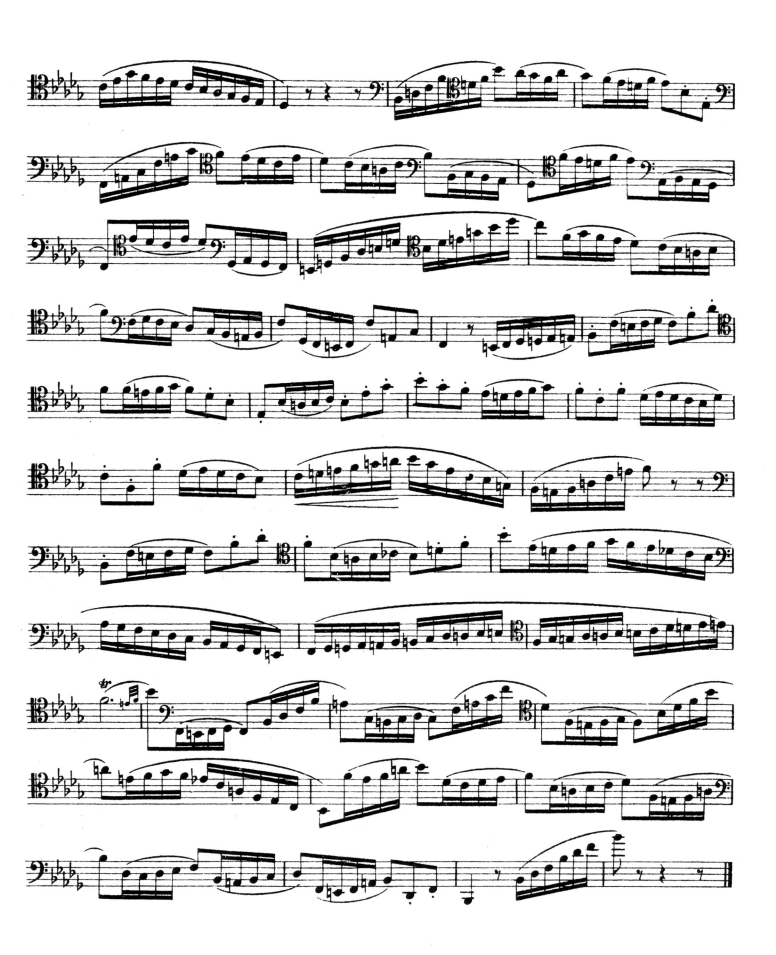

60

33.

Polonaise.

34.

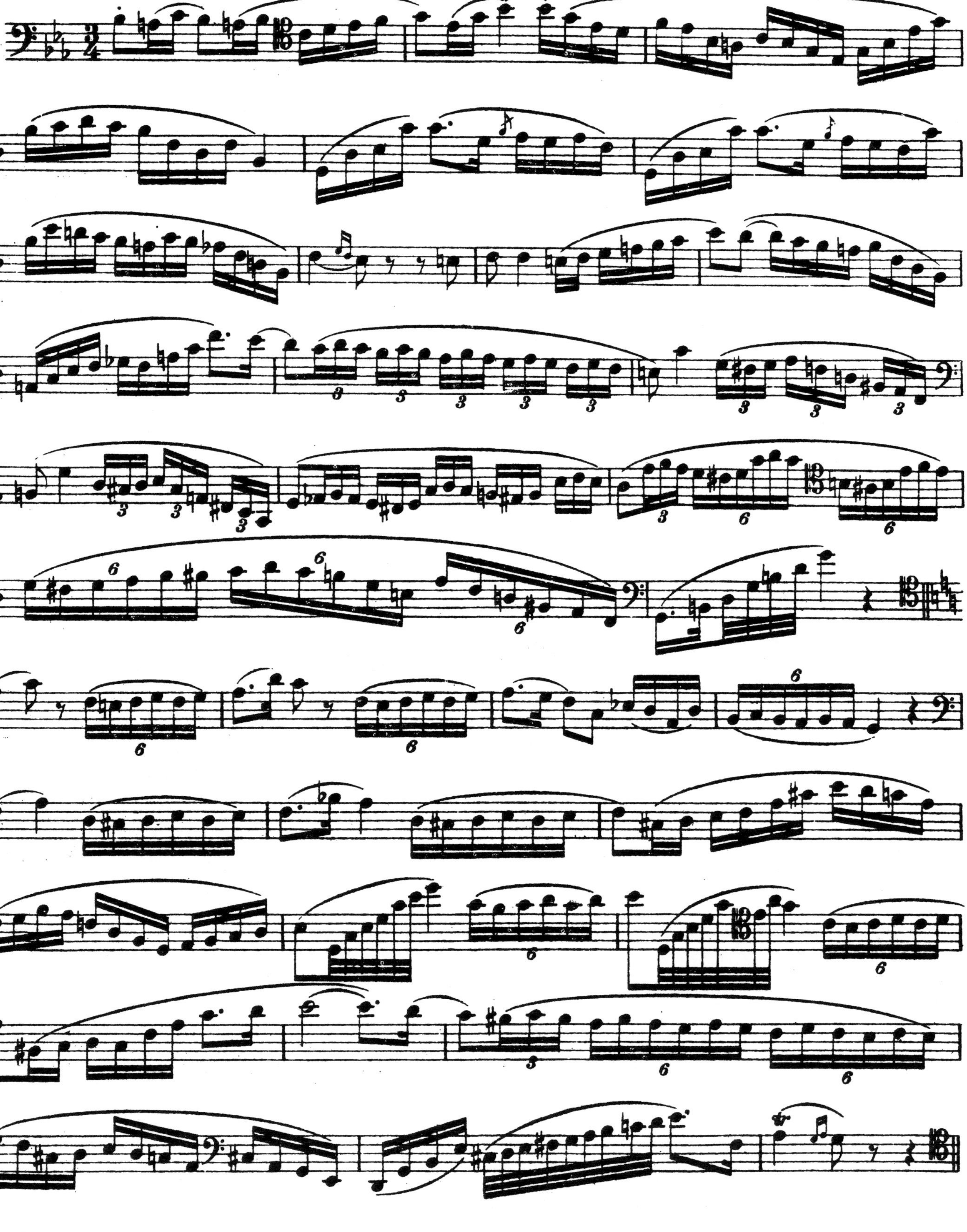

Polonaise D. C. al Fine.

66

68

Scherzo.
Allegro.

36.

69

Fine.

70

Cantabile.

Scherzo D.C. al Fine.

74

Capriccio.
Allegretto.

38.

Fine

D.C.al Fine.

39.

Adagio.

f Cantabile.

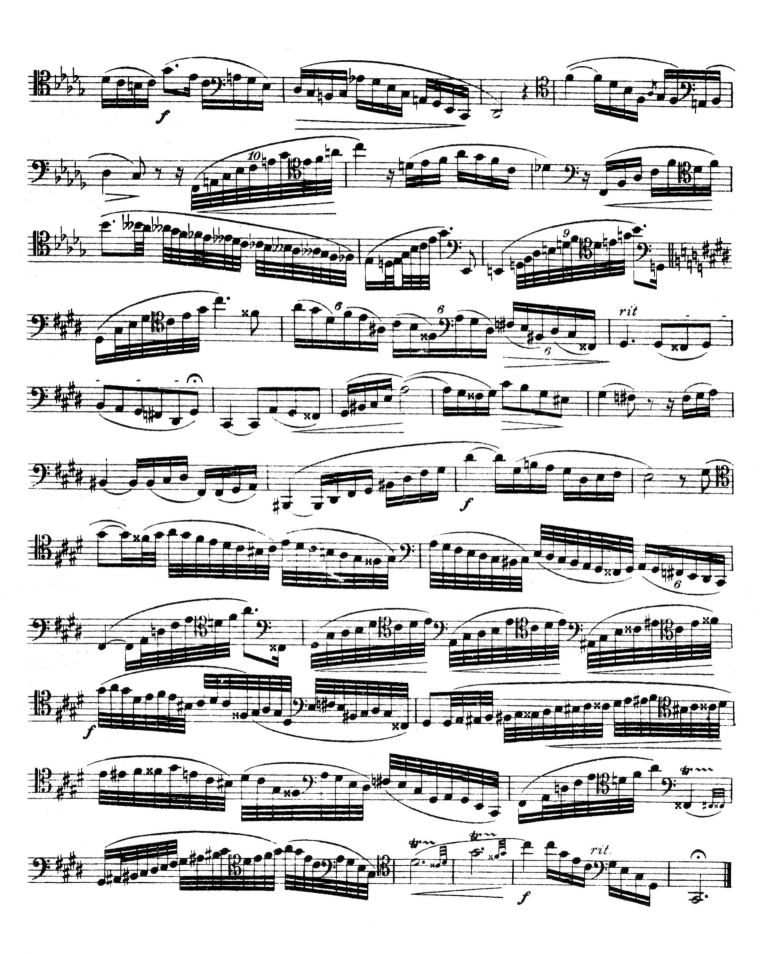

78

Capriccioso.
Presto.

40.

sempre stacc.

poco meno

80

Tempo I *(Allegro).*

Trio.

83

84

85

86

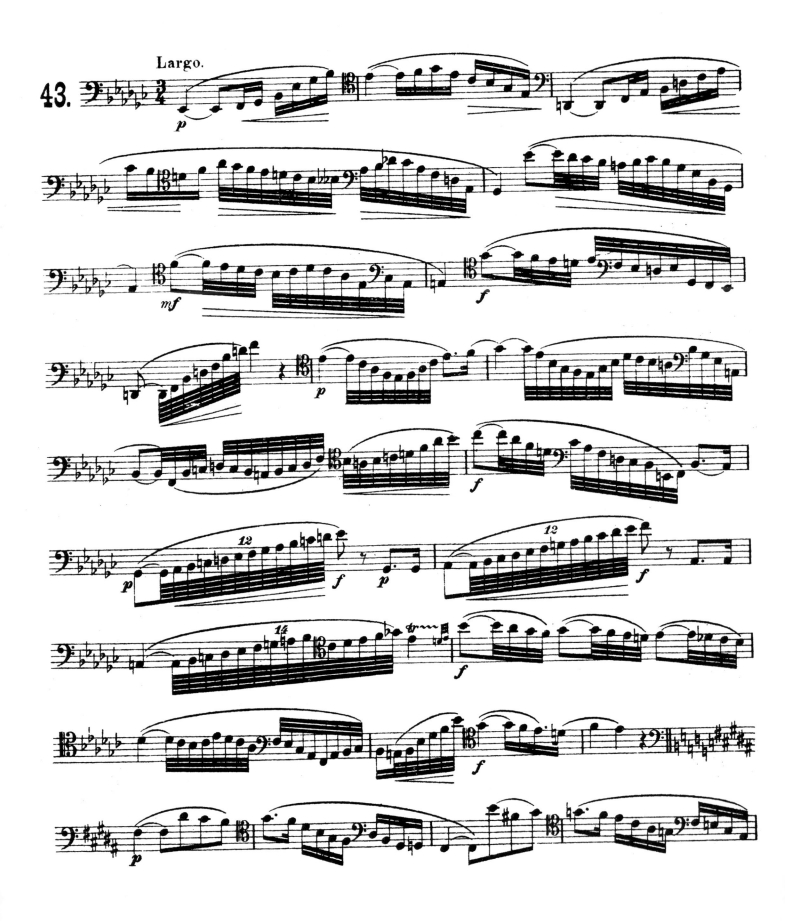

88

Moderato.

46.

94

95

49. Presto.

100